B.A.I. —
The Birmingham Athletic Ins

B.A.I.
THE BIRMINGHAM ATHLETIC INSTITUTE REMEMBERED

by

Charles Jenkins, Michelle Shoebridge
and Patricia Van Zyl

edited by

M. Irene Waterman

BREWIN BOOKS

First published
by Brewin Books, Studley, Warwickshire, B80 7LG
in November 1992

ISBN 1 85858 006 4

British Library Cataloguing in Publication Data.
A Catalogue record for this book is available from the British Library

Typeset in Baskerville by Avon Dataset, Bidford on Avon, Warwickshire, B50 4JH
and made and printed by The Cromwell Press, Broughton Gifford, Melksham, Wiltshire.

Acknowledgements

Our first debt is to Miss Waterman, who as the distinguished Principal of the Women's Section of the Birmingham Athletic Institute from 1944 – 1975 helped to make its history. Her advice and encouragement during the writing of this celebration was much appreciated. Her thesis "History of the Birmingham Athletic Institute" (1866 – 1918), provided an invaluable source for this work, as did her meticulous record-keeping during her time as Principal. We have relied heavily on this original study.

Our thanks are also due to Jimmy Munn who, as Director of Recreation & Community Services, first suggested the idea of a centenary history; to Carol Brown who carried out some initial work, offered support and encouragement throughout, and liaised between the various people involved; to Eric Bates and to Kerry Mumford, for their interest and advice; to Birmingham Public Libraries, Local Studies Department, for its generous and efficient assistance; to Karen Davies who remained patient and efficient throughout the typing of the manuscript, and to John Coates for helping with the proof reading.

Photograph acknowledgements to The Birmingham Post and The Sunday Mercury.

Charles Jenkins, Michele Shoebridge, Patricia van Zyl
The University of Birmingham
May 1989

PREFACE

"The best governed city in the world"

During the late 18th and early 19th centuries Birmingham was rightly famous as the workshop of the world, exporting goods all over Europe and North America. By the 1870's it was also becoming known as the best governed city in the world due to pioneering developments in local government. This civic revolution transformed municipal government and led to an improvement in the quality of life of the citizens of Birmingham. Radical changes in public health, housing, and public utilities had an effect on people's physical condition, whilst developments in education along with the provision of libraries, museums, parks and swimming pools, created intellectual and cultural opportunities.

The inspiration for these pioneering social reforms came from a group of men who had made their fortunes in a city where there was a great diversity of trades, few large factories, an abundance of skilled labour and the possibility of rising up the social scale with relative ease. Many of the famous Birmingham figures of this time were related by marriage, the Chamberlains, the Kenricks, the Rylands and the Martineau's, to name but a few. Not only did they work together in local government, but shared the same political and Non-Conformist beliefs.

The early history of the Birmingham Athletic Institute, including the events leading up to its foundation in 1889, is intimately connected with Birmingham's tradition of social reform and philanthropy. The same people who inspired civic development were involved in the founding of the BAI and were numbered amongst its most fervent benefactors during its early period. George Kenrick, George Dixon and Henry Mitchell were particularly associated with its foundation. Through their efforts the BAI was able to make a unique contribution to the history of physical education and sport in Britain.

This modest centenary history pays tribute to those men and women who placed physical education and health promotion through physical recreation high on their agenda; to the BAI which set the pattern for much of the country and to the generations of members whose lives were enriched by physical recreation.

CONTENTS

ORIGINS

In October 1889 a public meeting chaired by the Mayor of Birmingham, Francis Gordon-Clayton, proposed the establishment of an Institute of Higher Physical Education to be known as the Birmingham Athletic Institute. Thus was founded the BAI which was opened in John Bright Street by the Attorney General Sir Richard Webster in 1892.

This was not however the beginning of the story of the BAI, for by the 1840s, leading figures in the town were appalled by the effects that factory work and urban life were having on young people. To alleviate these effects the Young England Party founded the Athenic Institute in Suffolk Street to secure for its working class members the means for achieving mental, moral and physical improvement, together with rational amusement.

As a member of the society pointed out in 1844, the state of the working classes meant that education could only be afforded them through recreation and relaxation. Above all the labour of the people had to be curtailed to provide rest, relaxation and recuperation so that improvement in education could be secured by combining rational recreation and learning.

Inspired perhaps by the example of the Athenic Institute, a group of young men formed the Birmingham Athletic Club in 1866 to further gymnastics, athletics and all branches of physical culture. The club used the poultry bay in the Bingley Hall in which a room measuring 208′ × 57′ was made available and equipped with apparatus sufficient for 200 to exercise at the same time. The Club also took over the athletic grounds in Portland Road for cricket, athletics and football. A swimming club was started at the Kent Street Swimming Baths and paper chases were held during the winter.

Unfortunately space does not allow us to dwell on the achievements of the BAC under the leadership of Joseph Hubbard, an Old Edwardian who was the first paid instructor, later becoming Director with the title of Professor until 1896. Suffice it to say that under his leadership, and with the support of the Vice President, Clement Davies, the BAC led the country in providing classes, training leaders and in promoting physical education in schools some 12 years before physical education was included in the curriculum of elementary schools.

ORIGINS

By 1870 the Annual Report proclaimed, with justifiable pride "The Birmingham Athletic Club ... is the only institution which offers to the youth of this town a sound physical education. It is likely that before long physical education will form an essential part of general education in schools supported by public funds: then the value of your Club to the town will be incalculable".

And so it proved to be, not just to Birmingham, but to the country. Sir George Dixon MP, an athlete, dedicated supporter and member of the BAC and the first Chairman of the School Board, argued forcibly for the widening of the school curriculum to include physical education and urged amongst other things the provision of cheap children's passes to public swimming pools. George Dixon continued to campaign for the promotion of games and exercises in schools through his addresses to the School Board 1876 – 1886. In his 1881 address he claimed that:

"... Games and physical exercises ... improve attendance at school; attaches children to their respective schools and produces an honest pride in the lads of those schools which are victorious in matches. The practice of the game also takes the children away for a time from the crowded and unhealthy districts in which they live, and prevents them from becoming obnoxious to the people residing in the streets in which they would otherwise play ...

It is proposed to form a committee of gentlemen who take an interest in these exercises to stimulate the working of the clubs, and our new member George Kenrick has consented to act as Chairman. Should success continue to attend the movement, I hope that we shall be able to devise a plan for providing suitable exercises of an attractive nature for girls".

By November 1882 the School Board report noted that cricket clubs had been started in 25 schools with over 800 members and football clubs in 25 had attracted over 1000 members. Gymnastic apparatus had been provided in the schools and some 600 children were receiving instruction in the different exercise. It was reported in January 1883 that female teachers were receiving instruction in calisthenics and drill. At Dixon Road School the Headmistress had loaned her piano so that exercises could be performed more enjoyably to music. George Dixon, in his January report, looked forward to the time when all girls' schools could be provided with pianos. To promote the cause of physical education in schools George Dixon secured the formation of a

George Dixon M.P. Chairman of the School Board

George Kenrick
Chairman of the Council Birmingham Athletic Institute

Birmingham School Board Physical Exercises Committee in 1883 under the Chairmanship of George Kenrick. The objectives of the Committee were:

"1.   to give opportunity to every child to use its bodily powers to the fullest extent;

2.   to maintain the health and bodily strength of children by physical exercise corresponding to the mental activity required in their lessons;

4

3.   to develop a taste for all kinds of healthy exercise which may remain after school age and be a source of both health and pleasure throughout school life.''

By 1886 the Birmingham School board had accepted the proposals to introduce daily physical exercises in all schools and the Physical Exercises Committee was authorised to appoint a full time instructor to train the teachers and supervise their teaching. The scheme was approved by Her Majesty's Inspectorate. Sheffield, Leeds and Leicester soon followed Birmingham's example.

The Birmingham Athletic Club's contribution was emphasized in 1888 when Lord Beresford MP, Inaugural President of the National Physical Recreation Society, said in his speech at the annual demonstration of its work:

"Never in the history of empire was it more needful or more important that the people of England should be encouraged to pursue every sort of manual sport and exercise. The vast increase of machinery and other causes had driven a large number of people out of the country to the towns, and in the towns, both by nature of their employment and on account of the crowding of houses, they could not enjoy the fresh air and the exercise which was imperatively necessary for health and cheerfulness.

Every Englishman loved sport — every Englishman was moved by the spirit of emulation, desired some game which put him in condition and made him feel well ... such exercises as those carried out in the display would probably solve one of the great problems of the day — how to induce sobriety. Whoever embarked in athletics must exercise care and self-denial ... Athletics would do a vast amount of good to the factory. Activity of body produced activity of mind and activity of mind should be accompanied by activity of body.''

Lord Beresford went on to say that the people of Birmingham should feel proud of the achievements of the Club, "yet it laboured under its disadvantage of having premises which it had to vacate three or four times a year for other functions.'' Lord Beresford hoped that the town would make some effort to provide a piece of land:

".... whereon a gymnasium, not for 300, but for 3000 might be built. If Birmingham would support its Club according to its deserts then Birmingham would produce some splendid athletes.

FOUNDATION

Early in 1889 inspired by Lord Beresford's speech, the Birmingham Athletic Club suggested launching a city-wide appeal to raise funds to build a civic gymnasium for the citizens of Birmingham. Henry Mitchell, Chairman of the BAC opened the fund with a donation of £100 and many members subscribed. The BAC sought the support of the Mayor, Sir Thomas Martineau, who suggested names of prominent citizens who might be willing to help to raise the money.

However, in June 1889 Dr A. H. Carter, Senior Physician to the Queen's Hospital, and George Kenrick, who were both strong supporters of the BAC, asked to meet representatives of the BAC to discuss a scheme they had devised for the provision of athletic and gymnastics premises for the citizens of the town. George Kenrick was already active in promoting the cause of physical education in schools as a member of the School Board and Chairman of the physical Exercises Committee.

Dr Carter and George Kenrick convinced the representatives of the BAC that it would be possible to collaborate in the scheme, without prejudice to the interests of the Club. After prolonged discussion the Club Committee established a Special Committee which issued a Club Circular in October 1889 proposing the foundation of the Birmingham Athletic Institute. Early in 1890 the BAI General Committee issued a circular which defined the objectives of the Institute as follows:

''1.   To provide
   a) a large central gynmasium, fully equipped, a second hall and offices, committee room and reading room;
   b) four or more branch gymnasiums, hired in convenient parts of the city;
   c) playing fields under rules laid down by the Institute;

2.   To maintain a staff of instructors to teach:
   a) members of the BAC;
   b) teaching staff of the branch gymnasia;

Line drawing of BAI Premises 1889

c) those who wish to become teachers;

d) private individuals, classes or schools;

3.   To encourage:

a) the formation of boys' and girls' clubs in connection with public elementary schools and other bodies, for all kinds of exercises and games, by affording accommodation and advice, and possibly some money to get started.

b) healthy and desirable forms of physical exercise and recreation, by lectures, displays etc.''

Canvassing was vigorous during the spring and summer of 1890 and on 20th October subscribers were called to a meeting at the Council House with George Kenrick presiding. Of 1300 possible subscribers, 650 had been contacted of whom 360 had promised one guinea. At this meeting the report of the Canvassing Committee was approved and the Mayor, Alderman Clayton, moved that subscriptions should be considered due on 1 January 1891. The Sites and Buildings Sub Committee recommended an available site in John Bright Street for the new gymnasium to be erected at an estimated cost of £6,000.

The first Council of the Institute was then appointed under the presidency of Henry Mitchell who went on to serve in this capacity until his death in 1914. J. M. Hubbard was appointed as Director and Superintendent, with A. F. Aston, who had been trained at the Royal Training College for Gymnastic Teachers at Dresden, as first assistant on a three year engagement. The second assistant appointed was Charles Brodbeck, who had previously been teaching in Zurich where he had earned a considerable reputation as an expert gymnast and teacher of leaders in physical training. From the outset then, the BAI attracted a team of professional qualified teachers who had gained experience in Europe. This was over 40 years before Britain produced its own professionally qualified specialist teachers of physical education from Carnegie College, Leeds.

At the same meeting another decision was made which was to have important consequences for physical education and recreation, not just in Birmingham, but nationwide. This was the transfer of the responsibilities of the Birmingham School Board Physical Exercises Committee to the Birmingham Athletic Institute from 1 January 1891. Subsequently the Council of the BAI recommended the formation of a Committee of Management of

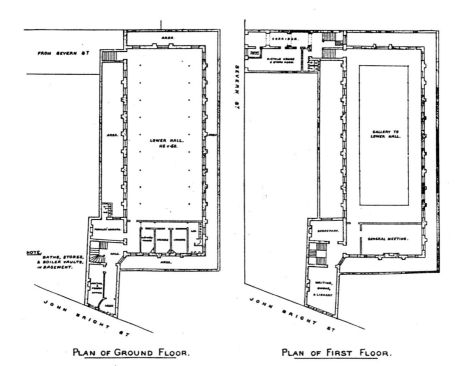

PLAN OF GROUND FLOOR. PLAN OF FIRST FLOOR.

Physical Exercises in Elementary Schools to comprise one of its members, four teachers from board schools and four teachers from denominational schools. The intention was, in the future, to provide city-wide coverage of school physical education, sports competitions and festivals.

However, the Council's ambitions for the Institute did not stop with the premises at John Bright Street, for George Kenrick and T. G. Lee had already purchased 29 acres of leasehold land adjacent to the Pershore Road and within easy reach of the BAI to be developed as playing fields. Nine benefactors agreed to pay the interest on the loan and to offer the land to the Council of the BAI for five years at a nominal rent. Development of the site was estimated to cost £1000, which it was hoped would be covered by public subscription. By the time of the official opening of the BAI £230 has been subscribed, but the playing fields proved to be a serious drain on the BAIs finances in the future.

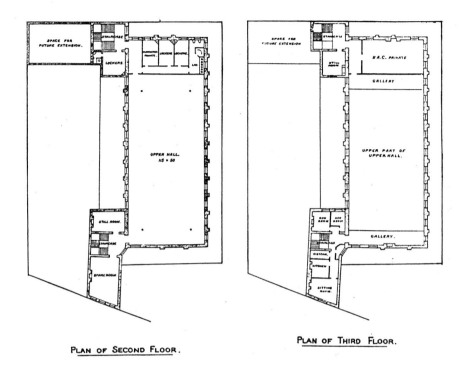

PLAN OF SECOND FLOOR.

PLAN OF THIRD FLOOR.

Original architects plans

The Official Opening

The official opening of the BAI by the Attorney General, Sir Richard Webster, was a gala occasion attended by a large and influential audience and widely reported in the press as indeed the sentiments expressed by Sir Richard and by Henry Mitchell deserved. The Birmingham Gazette's very full report of the event is included almost in its entirety.

The day before the official opening George Kenrick, who had built and furnished the premises at his own expense, informed the Council that it was his intention to lease it at a nominal rent in order to give the BAI time to become established. This act of generosity was only the first in his distinguished and lifelong service to the BAI.

The BAI gymnasium at John Bright Street was officially opened by Sir Richard Webster in February 1892. Supporters and members of the BAI were

11

Henry Mitchell President of the B.A.I. 1889-1914

somewhat anxious during the first year of operation at John Bright Street lest the Institute would be unable to pay its way. However, despite these anxieties over finance the Annual Report for 1892 was reassuring and optimistic. The gymnasium had been fully occupied during the evenings by the BAC on Tuesdays and Fridays, the YMCA on Mondays and Wednesdays and by public classes for youths and men on Thursdays and Saturdays. Full use of the

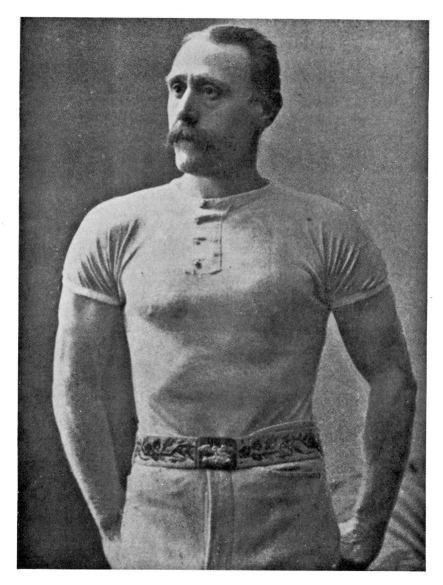

Prof Hubbard 1st Director & Superintendant B.A.I.

The actual building 1892

The large gymnasium 1892

building during daytime had proved difficult to achieve, but classes had been arranged for Post Office employees, middle-aged gentlemen, ladies (senior and junior), lady shop assistants, private classes for ladies and, significantly in relation to education, classes for school board female pupil teachers.

The School Board Report for 1892 recognised the value of the scheme.

"There can be no doubt that the physical exercises greatly improve the health and vigour of the pupil teachers and enable them to bear much more easily the amount of work which devolves upon them, both in schools and in the classes for their own instruction."

Anthropometric apparatus for measuring height and weight, lifting power-strength, lung capacity and reaction-time had been installed and was in full use. The laboratory was open to the general public on Monday and Thursday afternoons. Professor Windle was investigating the physical status of the female pupil teachers, all of whom were to be measured by the end of the first summer. Dr Carter was assessing the physical and health status of the lady shop assistants.

The Birmingham Athletic Institute Remembered

OPENING OF THE BIRMINGHAM ATHLETIC INSTITUTE

SIR RICHARD WEBSTER ON ATHLETIC TRAINING

On Saturday afternoon the Birmingham Athletic Institute was formally opened by the ATTORNEY GENERAL (Sir Richard Webster), in the presence of a large and influential gathering.

Mr HENRY MITCHELL presided at the opening ceremony, and was supported by Sir Richard Webster, the Mayor (Mr. Lawley Parker), the Bishop of Coventry, Mr. G. Dixon, M.P., Mr. W. Kenrick, M.P., the Rev. Canon Greeney, the Rev. E. F. M. MacCarthy, the Rev. H. F. Pegg, Miss Dale, Mr. J. C. Holder, Mr. J. H. Pearson, Mr. A. Keen, Mr. G. H. Kenrick, Councillors Beale, A. Dixon, Price, Lancaster, Walsh, and Winkles; Dr. Rickards, Messrs. E. L. Tyndall, J. B. Carslake, Lakin Smith, John Bowen, J. M. Hubbard (director), and J. Adams (secretary). Letters of apology were received from the Bishop of Worcester, the Right Hon. Henry Matthews, M.P., the Right Hon. J. Chamberlain, M.P., Sir Walter Foster, M.P., Mr. J. Dugdale, Q.C., M.P., Mr. H. Wiggin, M.P., Mr. J. A. Bright, M.P., Mr. Jesse Collings, M.P., Captain Grice-Hutchinson, M.P., Sir Thomas Martineau, Dr. Crosskey, Mr. C. E. Mathews, Mr. Sam Timmins, and others.

The CHAIRMAN remarked that everyone must recognise that health was the source of all physical happiness, and health could not be maintained without the proper cultivation of bodily powers. It was pleasant to see Birmingham again in the van of progress by the formation of that necessary and splendid institution, the work of which would favourably influence the physical welfare and social happiness of the inhabitants of this city. The institution would encourage and provide gymnastic exercises as well as facilities for football, cricket, swimming, and all outdoor sports from an amateur standpoint. Another of its aims would be the improvement of knowledge of the members on the management and preservation of health. Birmingham was indebted very greatly to Mr. G. H. Kenrick, Chairman of the Council of the Institute, who had nobly come forward and, by assuming the entire financial and working responsibilities, had converted a desirable ideal into an absolute reality — (applause).

SIR RICHARD WEBSTER said he esteemed it a great privilege to be permitted to snatch some hours from a somewhat fully-occupied life to pay a visit to Birmingham and have his name connected with the opening ceremony of such an institution — (hear, hear). Of the details of its work the audience had already heard, but he would like to lay before them some reasons which would induce the people and the Corporation of Birmingham to value an institution of that kind, and be proud that in that as in other matters Birmingham had been able to take the lead and show the way to neighbouring cities and towns. The subject was a very large and interesting one. From the point of view of the civilisation of the people, and from the point of view of the development of natural physical resources, the question was one of national importance — (hear, hear). In the present struggle for life the advantages of mental development or literary pursuits could not be underrated. They were as essential as ever. It was absolutely necessary for persons who had to make their way in life to be equipped with everything in the shape of mental resources and literary acquirements which the best education could give them; but in bygone days the importance of physical development, in order to get the best-trained and the best-framed bodies for the reception of mental instruction, had, perhaps, been a little overlooked. The experience of those who had studied the question and had been acquainted with the Swedish system was that a child with a well-nurtured or well-developed frame was better qualified to receive mental instruction or improvement. The idea used to prevail that from the point of view of physical development and instruction people had only to regard those individuals who were specially intended by nature to surprise their fellow-countrymen by their prowers. No greater mistake ever prevailed. The public ought not solely, or indeed mainly, to encourage those who by their natural gifts would become pre-eminent. It was those who had no incentive to win prizes or to astonish their fellow-countrymen who should be encouraged. General encouragement ought to be given to the rising generation to take regular and active exercise so that there might be a simultaneous growth of the body and development of the mind. He had been very much struck with the energy and foresight of the promoters of that institution. The names of several of the gentlemen had been mentioned, but, with characteristic modesty, the Chairman had omitted his own name, yet to Mr. Mitchell as much as to anyone the Institute was largely indebted — (hear, hear). Although that gymnasium was being inaugurated only that afternoon, the promoters were able to point to clubs started, gymnasia inaugurated, and training classes already in existence and doing good work in this thickly-populated city — (hear, hear). In Mr. Hubbard, the Institute possessed an excellent instructor—(applause)—and he (Sir Richard), after having for many years been interested in that kind of work in the east, north, and suburbs of London, had arrived at the conclusion that the service of a competent instructor could not be too highly valued. Many a man could do things, but it was not every one who could teach — (hear, hear). He heard with great satisfaction that classes were carried on for boys and girls after they had left the Board schools, for he could assure them that the interest and advantage attaching to gymnastic exercises did not cease when a boy or girl reached the age of fifteen or sixteen, but continued to develop for ten or fifteen years afterwards — (hear, hear). The control and organisation by the Institute of the classes at the schools was a commendable practice. If each of the forty or fifty elementary schools in Birmingham had its own system of instruction and rules, the result would be that not one-tenth of the value would be derived as was the case when, as at present, the direction proceeded from one central organisation which was in the position of hearing of and testing the latest developments in physical training. Thus it was of extreme importance that the Institute should be fostered and encouraged by all persons connected with elementary education, so that it might be an efficient director, controller, and guide of the games and athletic pursuits carried on in the minor and scattered schools in distant parts of the city. Much benefit also would result from the series of lectures on health, sanitation, and kindred subjects, which instruction was due entirely, it should be remembered, to the liberality of Mr. Mitchell — (applause). As for the building itself, he would not say it was the largest he had seen, because, having visited a number of gymnasia he had in his mind one or perhaps two which were a little larger, but in respect of its equipment and the accommodation for spectators the Birmingham Gymnasium was as complete, convenient, and commodious as any in existence, and was one of which the city might well be proud. Provision had been made by the architect, Mr. Corser, for the erection of another gymnasium over the present one, and in other directions the premises were capable of considerable extension. Remembering that the Institute had been secured to the inhabitants of Birmingham for five years free of cost, the debt of gratitude which was due to Mr. Kenrick was no small one — (applause). Valuable statistics would, no doubt, be compiled in the anthropometrical laboratory. He confessed he did not personally attach very much importance to that branch of the work, but that was, perhaps, because he did not understand it so well as he ought to — (laughter). The acquisition also, as the result of the free gift of nine gentlemen — (applause) — of thirty acres, to be used as playing fields, was one of immense value when the advantage accruing from the practice of outdoor sports was considered — (hear, hear). Mr. Mitchell had asked for additional subscribers to the Institute, and had expressed a fear lest the gymnasium should not be sufficiently popularised. Moreover, he drew a somewhat painful picture — or it appeared to him (Sir Richard) in that light when he remembered that all the running he was capable of nowadays was after an omnibus — (laughter) — of members of the Corporation disporting themselves on the parallel bars. Let the Chairman make no mistake! There would not be any room for members of the Corporation upon the parallel bars. Possibly, if the Mayor came down one evening the youth of Birmingham would stand aside while he set them an example — (laughter). One important point in connection with the instruction to be obtained at the Institute and the classes carried on under its suspices was that it was open to girls as well as boys — (hear, hear). Everybody knew what an enormous advantage it was to a girl to have active-exercise between the ages of nine and eighteen, and it added greatly to the interest of men and women when witnessing an athletic display of any kind if in their younger days they had taken part in the same exercises or pursuits It was impossible to overstate the value to the poor girls in the East of London of the opportunities of pleasurable exercise such as were afforded in the gymnasia there. The difference of expression upon a child's face after an hour's course of exercises with her playmates was really remarkable, and he was certain it made her life brighter and happier — (hear, hear). It was not necessary that the benefits of such an institution should be confined to one particular class, and the promoters did not desire or intend that they should be — (hear, hear). Certain hours each day were set apart for persons belonging to what were termed the middle classes, and almost the whole day through the gymnasium would be occupied with classes of one kind or another. He noticed that a class for middle-aged men had been started. The promoters of the Institute had wisely stated that they did not draw the line — they did not say where middle-age began — (laughter). He was afraid that if they had laid down any strict regulations regarding age, a little difficulty would have been experienced in extracting from some of the gentlemen the date of their first birthday — (laughter). It was a great satisfaction to him to see how well the whole scheme had been thought out by the founders and promoters of the institute; and he predicted that long before five years had passed they would not only, by reasons of the support accorded them, hold that institution and the playing fields, but that they would have sufficient funds to carry out extensions. There was a still wider and, if he might so term it, deeper aspect in which the question might be regarded, and that was the commingling of all classes of the community which took place at a gymnasium. In the Badminton volume on "Skating" there was a chapter on curling, a popular Scottish pastime, concerning which a good story was told: A blacksmith was travelling third class to a curling matoh. "I see," said a companion, "you are drawn against the laird." "Oh!" was the reply, "I shall be laird of him to-night" — (laughter). Such sports brought people together with a common interest, and showed that, after all, they were members of one big family — (hear, hear). It had also a humanising influence; it taught a man to go to another who had beaten him and say, "Well done, old fellow," making him feel proud of having been defeated by one who was better than himself. Athletic exercises brought together all sorts and conditions of men and caused them to smile and forget those differences which, on other platforms, sometimes occasioned ill-will and unfriendliness. He believed that in promoting such institutions, founded on the

lines on which that one had been established, the prime movers in the matter were really forwarding one of the most useful works which could be promoted in the physical and mental education of the young people of this country; and for that reason, if none other, he was proud of having been permitted to assist in that ceremony — (hear, hear). In declaring the Birmingham Athletic Institute open, he, in the name of all lovers of athletic sports, wished it a bright and prosperous career — (applause). He hoped that before many years had passed even that fine building would grow too small for the number of persons who desired to reap the advantage of the instruction which would be given there. He could not wish everyone who competed to be a winner, but he could hope that in all the contests, from beginning to end, there would always be fair play — (hear, hear) — and he sincerely trusted, in fact he firmly believed, that the Institute would prove a blessing to Birmingham, and would be a credit to everyone who had been associated with its foundation (applause).

The BISHOP of COVENTRY moved a vote of thanks to the Attorney-General for his attendance and services.

Mr. G. H. KENRICK, in seconding the motion, said that athletic exercise would do more to empty the hospitals and keep them empty than all the drugs in the city — (laughter and hear, hear). The Council was glad they had provided for Mr. Hubbard a permanent home where he would not be interrupted by the lowing of oxen or the cackling of fowls — (laughter). He wished he could say that they had also provided a place of rest for their indefatigable secretary, but all that they had been able to find him up to the present was more work than he had ever had to do before — (laughter) — and to those people who knew Mr. Adams that meant a very great deal indeed — (applause).

The vote was accorded and acknowledged.

The MAYOR, in proposing a vote of thanks to the Chairman, remarked that it might be necessary for him to avail himself of the offer to practice on the parallel bars, for, to his astonishment, he had found on being weighed the previous day in London, that he scaled more than he had ever done — (laughter).

Mr. W. KENRICK, M.P., who seconded the proposition, mentioned that the School Board, recognising the good work which the Institute was doing amongst the school children, had resolved to contribute to its funds a sum of £250 a year in order that the female pupil teachers might not only profit by the exercises, but be taught them so thoroughly as to be able to impart the knowledge to the school girls. His own daughters were attending the Institute classes, and deriving great benefit from the exercise, and he strongly recommended the young ladies of Birmingham to follow their example — (hear, hear, and laughter).

The proposition was carried, and, the CHAIRMAN having replied, the proceedings ended.

In the evening a gymnastic display took place, the building being thronged with spectators. Sir RICHARD WEBSTER, who presided, congratulated the members of the Institute on their new home. He proceeded to urge the desirability of the attainment of a general level of merit in performances rather than the excellence of individual pupils, and concluded by reminding the members how deeply they were indebted to Mr. Kenrick, Mr. Mitchell, and Dr. Carter — (applause).

At the close a vote of thanks was, on the motion of the Rev. A. B. VARDY, seconded by the Rev. N. M. HENNESSY, accorded the Chairman.

The ATTORNEY-GENERAL, in replying, described the entertainment as a splendid one, and said he had never seen exercises better performed, or pupils doing greater credit to their teachers — (applause).

The musical accompaniments to the exercises were played by Mrs. Hubbard.

THE INSTITUTE TIME TABLE. 1892

	9-30 to 11	11-30 to 1	3 to 4-30	5-30 to 7	7-30 to 9-30
MONDAY - - -	PUPIL TEACHERS (4th Year)		LADIES (SENIOR)	BOYS	YOUTHS AND MEN
TUESDAY - - -	PUPIL TEACHERS (Candidates)		LADIES (JUNIOR)	SENIOR GENTLEMEN	B.A.C.
WEDNESDAY - -	PUPIL TEACHERS 3rd Year)		YOUTHS, MEN, AND POST OFFICE A. C.	LADY SHOP ASSISTANTS	YOUTHS AND MEN
THURSDAY - -	PUPIL TEACHERS (2nd Year)		LADIES (JUNIOR)	BOYS	YOUTHS AND MEN
FRIDAY- , - -	PUPIL TEACHERS (1st Year)	YOUTHS, MEN, AND POST OFFICE A. C.	LADIES (SENIOR)	SENIOR GENTLEMEN	B.A.C.
SATURDAY- - -			*LADY TEACHERS AND THEIR FRIENDS	BOYS	YOUTHS AND MEN

* Not held in the Summer Term.

READING & WRITING Room open daily for the use of Subscribers.

1st programme of activities

The branch classes which had been opened at Floodgate Street, Foundary Road, Camden Street and Stratford Road proved to be most successful during this first year, remaining open and fully subscribed until May. The Saturday class for ladies at Stratford Road proved to be particularly successful, with attendance exceeding all expectations. The evening classes which were initially open to youths and men were extended by popular demand and it was decided to run separate classes for boys earlier in the evening. This proved an instant success in enrolling more young men and by the third class they had reached the target limit of 100 pupils.

Following a gift of books by a friend of the Institute the BAI Council laid the foundation for the development of the Institute Library. It also took the important initiative which was to establish a series of lectures on physical hygiene and health to be given each year by a competent professor to satisfy a great need in the education of young men. To achieve this Henry Mitchell offered an annual sum of £200. The lectures were so well attended that the City Council considered making arrangements to hold similar classes and lectures in different parts of the city.

18

Nearly one hundred years later the titles of the first four lectures given in 1892 address issues that still engage our attention. We still confront the problems of the health divide in large towns. We have at last recognised the value of physical activity and active lifestyles as counter-agents to the sedentary pursuits of urban populations and we still do not understand fully the mystery or the wisdom of the body. Despite the success enjoyed by the BAI in its first year the balance sheet for 1892 showed a deficit of £94.19s 9d and the Council of the BAI was concerned.

FROM PRIVATE ENTERPRISE TO PUBLIC OWNERSHIP

In 1989, the year in which the present government prepared a bill to put out local authority leisure facilities to competitive tender, it is ironic that we recall with pride the period in which the BAI passed from private ownership into local authority control.

Despite running a full and popular programme the balance sheets for 1893 and 1894 showed a deficit and in 1894 it was decided to appoint a full time Deputy Director to supervise daytime classes, which Professor Hubbard, who by now was employed full time at King Edward's School, was unable to do.

The BAIs appointment of Professor Clease as Deputy Director and ultimately as successor to Professor Hubbard proved to be a wise decision. By 1896, when the first five year lease expired, the balance sheet was in credit £36.10.8. This was due to the huge popularity of cycling classes.

In June 1896 the BAI presented the first all ladies display at the Town Hall which contemporary accounts describe as receiving a tremendous reception. The popularity of the BAI's work with women members continued to grow and the developments attracted national interest. For example, in March 1898, a team of young ladies under the director of Professor Clease travelled to Dublin to give a series of gymnastic and athletic displays to stimulate interest in physical education amongst young women and girls. This visit was made under the personal patronage of Countess Plunkett, who was later associated with the 1916 Irish uprising. The girls were magnificently received and the Irish public found it difficult to believe that the performers were amateur gymnasts and not members of a professional troupe! Following the success of this visit the BAI established regular gymnasts competitions for ladies.

The prominence given to women's physical training in the period 1894 – 1898 was pioneering work for, in addition to classes for female pupil teachers, weekly classes were also held for practising female teachers under the direction of S Bott, the School Board's Physical Education Supervisor. The course of instruction was designed to meet the Education Code's requirements and in 1896 the Department of Education officially recognised the BAI as a training centre for Teachers of Physical Exercises in Elementary Schools with authority to grant certificates to members who reached a fixed standard of efficiency.

The examination for the certificate comprised three branches of study — a written section on the physiology of exercise; a practical test performing a number of fundamental exercises to a high standard; a teaching test to show aptitude and sensitivity in handling children. The courses were popular and during 1898 45 candidates obtained the Teachers' Training Certificate in Physical Education.

The BAI partnership with the Education Authority also flourished through the work of the Physical Exercises Committee for Elementary School Children, which had been formed to organise out-of-school games and sports. Many local businessmen donated cups and shields for individual, team and school events including F W Harrold for swimming competitions; Warwick County Cricket Club for the Bocker Cricket Shield and the Birmingham District Counties Football Association for the Football Challenge Shield. In 1897 the first annual sports display by children attracted 750 boys and girls and in 1898 the Board of Education produced a full length report of the Institute's scheme for the organisation of extra-curricular games, recommending that other industrial cities would do well to follow suit.

1897 proved to be an important year in other ways. The credit balance on the year's account had increased to £346.2s 1d, 1405 members had enrolled during the year and the BAI and the BAC collaborated to take part in the Birmingham Jubilee procession. Professor Clease and a Charles Brodbeck arranged for two floats to be designed as miniature gymnasia. One float had parallel bars on which 12 men in athletic costumes demonstrated exercises and the other displayed physical training exercises, weightlifting and boxing exercises. The Athletic Club's float displayed the trophies won by the club, which were insured for £200.

By this time physical exercises were enjoying a popularity boom in the Midlands and nationally. MPs, educationists and industrialists were stressing the importance of healthy physical pursuits. Small gymnastic clubs were literally "springing up all over the Midlands" and in 1899 the Midland Counties Amateur Gymnastics Association was founded to co-ordinate the work of Midlands clubs and to raise standards generally. In response to the city-wide growth in the numbers of amateur gymnasia the BAI equipped one of its rooms for remedial gymnastics for the treatment of physical and postural defects including curvatures, narrow chests, weak joints and obesity.

The free health lectures inaugurated in 1892, continued to be popular with the venues being changed systematically so that people from all areas of the city could attend. Titles of the lectures, for example those held in 1896, included: Cycling as an exercise; Indigestion and its causes; The care of the skin; Home nursing; Sleep and sleeplessness and, just to show that gender rules, *"Like father — like son"* — for men only!

The annual report for 1896 noted:

> "The large and enthusiastic audiences which have assembled for every lecture, not only bear witness to the appreciation of the work which is being done by the Institute in this direction, but justifies the hope that the work is bearing good fruit and will in time exercise a favourable influence upon the health of the city. There can be no doubt as to the great need of work of this kind and it supplements, we venture to think, the work of the Health Committee of the City Council to an important extent".

By the turn of the century the BAI had established itself and was playing an important part in education through teacher training and the promotion of extra-curricular activities in elementary schools, in community sport and physical training and in the general area of health promotion and health education.

Despite these achievements the BAI was operating at a loss of £64, which had risen to £329.4s.8d by 1901. The reserve fund was also seriously depleted. Membership had fallen to 117 each paying one guinea. There were 16 life members and four special subscribers. It is interesting to note from the list of members that most lived in Edgbaston and other upper and middle class enclaves of the city. In 1900 there were only two women members, Miss Edith Harrold, sister of one of the prizegivers and Miss Martineau, who came from one of the prominent Birmingham families. The time for women's membership of fitness clubs as a commonplace occurrence had yet to come, although there were a considerable number of women attending the classes on a casual basis. The decline in membership was attributed to the Boer War, economic depression, the opening of similar institutions within the city and inevitable contraction after a period of expansion. This pattern of decline was to continue throughout the early years of the century.

The health lectures continued to attract a sizable audience. Most lecturers employed were doctors and included Mary Sturge, grand-niece of the prominent Birmingham political figure, Joseph Sturge. Their subjects continued to range from men only sessions on sexual matters, practical

Lawrence Levy English & International Weight Lifting Champion 1891

sessions about physiology and diseases, to rather esoteric subjects which seem strange to us now — 'Clothing' — the structure of the skin; its uses. Why are clothes necessary? Materials. 'Practical suggestions', was the title of one particular session. They were aimed at educating the working classes in better health and hygiene. The external teaching undertaken by staff at the BAI brought in a little income. In 1901 staff taught in Wolverhampton, the Deaf and Dumb Institute, Graham Street Dissenting School and Brierley Hill Athletic School. Foreign contracts continued with some staff visiting the Swiss National Gymnastic fete at Chaux of Fons and a gymnastic competition in Paris. The BAI also continued to do good work in the elementary schools, under the supervision of Lawrence Levy. The competitions they organized ranged from gymnastics to running, jumping and swimming.

However, the area that had disappointed the BAI Council most was its failure to make money from private tuition in the gymnasium. The facilities on offer were:

"private gymnasium open for fencing, boxing, wrestling and broadsword exercises and for the treatment of weakliness, narrow chests, deformities and obesity under medical advice.

Defensive work, with the use of developing machines, 30/- for 12 lessons.

Private exercises for ladies and gentlemen £3.00 per annum. Special cases 5/- per lesson. Any with a weakness by arrangement".

In 1902 the BAI's long-term champion, George Kenrick, was elected Chairman of the newly formed Education Committee. He continued in this role for 18 years. His active involvement in the BAI continued and in 1904 he installed electric light in the gymnasium. This was much appreciated as it enabled activities to be carried out in a better light and purer air. In 1906 he defrayed the cost of lavatory alterations and the installation of four showers which seemed a considerable act of faith since the BAI continued to lose money and dip into its reserves. Occasionally fees were increased, but only resulted in membership falling off. In the same way, if rental charges for the Pershore Road football pitches were raised bookings fell. Parts of these playing fields were in bad repair, often made worse by acts of vandalism. They were a constant drain on the BAI's finances, costing approximately £40 a year to maintain. The extension of the tram line to Selly Park in 1904 raised hopes that their value would be enhanced by this ease of communication. However, by 1910, competition from the free hire of football pitches by the Parks Department forced the BAI to relinquish use of the fields to offset the general deficit.

1902 ended on a high note when in December the Lord Chief Justice of England, Lord Alverstone, who as Sir Richard Webster, had presided over the official opening of the Institute, made an unannounced and unexpected visit. Members of the Institute were delighted at this affirmation of his continuing interest in physical education and in work of the Institute. The newly appointed Director of the Institute, Staff Sergeant Hill quickly organised a special demonstration watched from the balcony by the Lord Chief Justice and George Kenrick. Lord Alverstone complimented the participants and thanked them for mounting such an impressive display at short notice. The Birmingham Daily Gazette noted on 17th December that ''His Lordship regretted that he could not be on the floor with the gymnasts''.

The 1903 Annual Report comments on the lack of continuity in staff. Charles Brodbeck, who had been with the Institute since its inauguration, had left the previous year to become Director of Physical Exercises under the Nottinghamshire School Board. Other staff joined the exodus, making continuity in classes difficult. There was a general ''falling off'' in afternoon classes and private tuition and the only new significant classes introduced were fencing for girls and ladies. Swimming had become an important element in the work for schools, free passes being awarded by the City Baths Committee for those who learnt to dive and swim 30 yards.

In 1905 special classes were set up for employees of the Post Office and Police Force and members of the Old Edwardians Football Club and Warwickshire County Cricket Club. It is difficult to assess how much money was made from these arrangements. It was generally acknowledged that the BAI's classes were expensive in comparison with others being run in the City possibly because they provided more equipment. The Institute also ventured into the martial arts with the introduction of classes in ju-jitsu. It seems they were ahead of their time because the 1907 report comments that ju-jitsu had not caught on. December 1906 saw the transfer of the classes for female pupil teachers to a new centre in Oozells Street after a period of 10 years. Performance in gymnastics in that year had been hampered by some of the best men having to leave the area for business reasons. However, Walter Tysall did win the individual Championship. He also won the Midland Counties Amateur Gymnastic Association prize the next year and was ranked the best amateur gymnast in the country. On the schools front, the interest in swimming continued. In efforts resembling those of our own Sports Council,

The Birmingham Athletic Institute Remembered

Birmingham Athletic Institute Team 1910
Thrice Winners of the Adams Shield

Massed display of Physical Exercises 1910

the City Baths Sub-Committee tried to encourage young people not to drop out of sport by issuing free swimming passes for a two year period after leaving school.

In 1908 the Committee were hoping for increased attendance at classes as a result of the Act for the Medical Inspection of Children. The merits of physical instruction were highlighted in an extract from the Graham Street Charity School Report of 1907:

"The Committee have again to thank Miss Edith Harrold for enabling the children to attend the Athletic Institute, and take this opportunity of making special mention of the physical development of the girls and the very marked benefit received from Mr Well's instruction ... the increase in height and weight of the children is very perceptible, so many having been admitted to the school stunted in growth and in bad condition generally."

Miss Harrold took an active interest in the BAI and was responsible for the introduction of Swedish gymnastics. Although not immediately successful it was not long before the classes became very popular.

1908 was also an Olympic Year and saw the BAI involved in both the organization and competitive side of this prestigious event. Lawrence Levy was appointed to the Olympic Council, H. E. Williams acted as Chief Steward and two members were judges in the Drill competitions. On the competitive side Walter Tysall, the BAI's star gymnast, came second in the Heptathlon, being narrowly beaten by Albert Braglia of Italy. It is interesting to note that a letter of protest stated the choice of judges should have been made with a neutral bias instead of being all British. Walter Tysall's medal is the only individual Olympic medal ever won by a British gymnast. Samuel Hodgetts came sixth in this event, and the Institute also contributed to the gymnastics and wrestling teams.

The 1909 Annual Report opened by setting out the dire financial position. The previous year had seen an increase in fees for classes. This had been partially successful in the more popular classes, but the overall result was a loss of income and they were reduced to their original level. Although rental of the Pershore Road playing fields had ceased, the general deficit still stood at £1,102.11s.10d. Despite its financial problems the Institute won the Adams Shield making it the Champion Gymnastics Club of the British Isles. This success was repeated in the following year.

The Birmingham Athletic Institute Remembered

A major departure in the Institute's activities occurred in 1910 when the health lectures were discontinued. Henry Mitchell, long time benefactor of the lectures, suggested this because of the general improvement in the standard of health education. A limited programme, catering for men and women's topics separately, was instigated. The Committee commented on their worth:

"Favourable notice of our work by Mr A D Acland, at one time Minister of Education, led to health-teaching being introduced to our Elementary Schools as an optional subject, becoming subsequently an integral part of the curriculum in the upper Standards through the Schools of this country"

Drastic action regarding the financial situation was taken in 1911 when George Kenrick and Henry Mitchell agreed to clear the BAI's overdraft and persuaded a number of local businessmen to pay £50 for the following 5 years. These were Messrs W M & H A Butler, Messrs A B & C B Holinsworth, the BAC, A W Cadbury, J Barham Carslake, Edward Ansell and John Adams. This enabled the building to acquire new Swedish apparatus and a small gym fitted out for golf coaching. The evening Swedish Gymnastics classes for girls benefited greatly from the new equipment. The BAI also started running 12 month courses on the Hygiene and Physical Training Syllabus for the Certificate Examination Elementary Level. Classes took place on Saturday mornings for students from Saltley Training College and Birmingham Male Day Training College Teachers.

1912 was the first year for a long time that the BAI showed a small profit, bolstered as it was by the special subscriptions and increased membership in all classes, especially in those for women's classes, senior and girls. It was also active in competition supplying six members of the team of 24 gymnasts who competed in the Olympic Games in Stockholm and in organizing an Athletic Festival at St Andrews in which 2,380 girls and boys competed. One of the Institute's past prize winners, Walter Tysall was appointed Director of the Northampton Athletic Club.

It was not long before financial problems began to plague the BAI again, with a deficit of £32 by 1913. The advent of the First World War did not as can be imagined, help. Initially the Committee thought the war would be shortlived. They talked of "temporary staff difficulties", and "falling membership" but soon, many BAI and BAC names were being added to the Roll of Honour.

During the war two important figures associated with the BAI died. Henry Mitchell, President and Treasurer since the BAI was founded, died at the beginning of the War. No mere figurehead, he had contributed considerable time and money to the BAI. His son, Arthur Mitchell, was appointed to follow him as President, although initially he was serving abroad. In 1916 Professor Hubbard, the first teacher at the BAC and long associated with the BAI, died. He had been ill for two years, and in 1915 had received a testimonial collection of £250 from the BAC.

By 1915 membership had dropped dramatically with an estimated 280 BAI members enlisted along with 70 BAC members. Many women joined the voluntary organisations including citizens and relief committees. Air raids and lighting restrictions interfered with those evening classes that did run. Despite this the BAI continued classes and the next Annual Report illustrated how they thought they could contribute after the War. George Kenrick commented that:

> "the lessons learnt in the War would emphasize the great necessity of an institution of that kind, and he had no doubt our men would come home realising how essential it was they should keep themselves in a state of the highest physical efficiency and that the institute afforded one of the best means of doing it ... never before had so urgent a call been made on the physical endurance of British manhood and it is confidently believed that the large majority of the 60,000 soldiers the city had supplied are physically stronger and more amenable to military duties and discipline because of their athletic training at school."

By 1917 the Birmingham Post reported that although the BAI and BAC were losing money they had:

> "further demonstrated their usefulness ... by additional contributions of fit athletic men for the colours ... It was gratifying to hear from the men themselves that the work at the Institute gymnasium accelerated their army training, hastened efficiency, and in many cases helped forward rapid promotion".

The BAI was in a very bad financial state and could no longer count on the support of the businessmen who had backed it for five years. The BAC was contributing to the losses because of its falling membership. However, George Kenrick was reluctant to see the BAI close when the end of the War was

30

imminent. He had been associated with it for 25 years and in 1917 received a framed photograph from Lawrence Levy, Chairman of the BAC, who made a speech in praise of his contribution to the development of physical education. By the beginning of 1918 rumours abounded that the BAI would be forced to close and the Birmingham Post carried a feature predicting this. Closure was deferred by George Kenrick offering the building in John Bright Street and the playing fields on the Pershore Road to the City. No conditions were attached to the gift, but it was suggested that the Education Committee should use the building to introduce some of the provisions laid down for physical training in the Fisher Education Bill. At the final meeting of its Council, George Kenrick expressed regret at severing almost 30 years connection but he realised the future of the Institute would be far more secure under the Education Committee.

FROM STRENGTH TO STRENGTH

Thus the BAI entered a new phase, but narrating its history from the transfer to the Birmingham Education Committee until the 1930's when annual reports were written again, has proved a difficult task. The affairs of the BAI occur occasionally in the Education Committee Minutes, in the Technical Education and Evening Schools Sub Committee, which took responsibility for the continuation of the evening classes, and later in the Reports of the Sites and Buildings Sub-Committee. The latter is mainly concerned with staffing. Along with the changes in ownership an agreement was made with the BAC whereby it could continue to use the Institute on certain evenings and have the use of a room and office, all for a rent of £100 a year. This caused continuing problems for the BAI, which attempted to terminate the tenancy on several occasions, especially when the success of the classes meant they were very short of space. By 1922 an amicable agreement had been reached whereby the club retained possession of the gymnasium, but gave up the Club Room.

During the 1920's and early 1930's the teachers at the BAI were employed on a part-time basis with duties at other schools. In January 1924 A Trevillian was appointed physical education teacher at the Kings Norton Secondary School, Handsworth Technical School and the Athletic Institute, on a salary of £215 a year. By 1930 the salary had risen to £246 with the appointment of John Milne. In 1935 – 36 the BAI employed 17 women members of staff, 6 of whom were pianists. In 1936 the headship was given increased hours at the BAI, in recognition of the responsibility associated with running the Centre, and the huge number of classes and enrolments. By this time J B Clark was the full-time head.

1937 was a particular milestone for the BAI because it was finally divided into two departments and a women's headmistress appointed to oversee the women's classes. This was very much the result of a report written by Anne Thorpe, the Organizing Inspector of Physical Training for the City of Birmingham, who had been appointed in the early 1930's. Her influence and interest, especially in physical recreation for women, was to prove very useful to the BAI. J B Clarke, the retiring headmaster, fully supported the appointment, having realised that he did not have the time or the technical

CITY OF BIRMINGHAM EDUCATION COMMITTEE

Birmingham Athletic Institute
JOHN BRIGHT STREET

SESSION 1930-31

EVENING CLASSES IN
PHYSICAL
TRAINING

Head Teacher:
MR. J. M. MILNE

The next term will commence on
12TH JANUARY, 1931.

N

1931 Programme of Activities

Mrs Eileen Harper leading an afternoon class for women 1937

expertise to develop the women's side. Although the demand was there for women's classes, they were not growing as fast as the men's. In 1930 – 34 the men's classes doubled, but the women's enrolments only increased from 559 to 609. It was felt that a woman head could decide which classes were needed, work out technical details, advise on dress and hygiene and set a standard (at an advanced level) both for the BAI and the City. In addition swift action was needed to counter the popular, cheap classes being run by the League of Health and Beatuy, the Everywomen's Health Movement and private dancing classes. The first women's Head, Mrs Eileen Harper, had been a part-time teacher at the Institute, and she proved to be a very enthusiastic and skilful leader.

The very popularity of the BAI at this time brought space problems. By 1932 – 33 there was a further increase in students and in the number of classes

Extracts from 1937 Syllabus

CITY OF BIRMINGHAM EDUCATION COMMITTEE

TRAINING COURSE FOR WOMEN
LEADERS OF RECREATIVE PHYSICAL
TRAINING

Commencing 17th January, 1938

ENROLMENT FORM

Name (in Block Capitals) .....

Address .,.........................

....

....

Voluntary Organisation with v

... .

....

Applicants are asked to state s
(if any) in practical physical t
recreation.

....

....

....

....

To be returned, not later than
P. D. Innes, Chief Educat
Margaret Street, Birminghar

CITY OF BIRMINGHAM EDUCATION COMMITTEE

A

TRAINING COURSE

for Girls and Women wishing to become

LEADERS

OF

Recreative Physical Training

in Clubs and other Organisations

will be held at the

UPPER HIGHGATE ST. GYMNASIUM

(Leopold Street, off Moseley Road)

on

Monday Evenings, 7.45—9.30 o'clock

commencing Monday, 17th January, 1938

Fee 5/- for the Course of 20 Sessions

TRAINING IN LEADERSHIP IN

| Keep Fit Exercises | Games | Swimming |
| Dancing (including Tap) | Skipping | Camping, Etc. |

A splendid opportunity for YOU to take part in the
National Fitness Campaign

P. D. INNES,
Chief Education Officer

Education Office
Margaret Street
Birmingham 3

P56050–B16 (a)

Advertisement for the first Leaders' Training Course 1938

TWO-YEAR PART-TIME TRAINING COURSE
for
Young Women Leaders of Physical Recreation
COMMENCING AUTUMN, 1946.

APPLICATION FORM

1. Name .... Date of Birth............
(BLOCK CAPITALS, SURNAME FIRST)
2. Address ....
....

3. School(s) where educated ....
....

4. Occupation (if still at school state wl
....
....

5. Particulars of any successes in Swimn
Athletics, Games etc., at school or l
....

6. Experience of Physical Recreati
(indoor and outdoor) ....
....

7. Particulars of experience as a lead
....

8. Is your health record good? ...

9. Observations, if any ....
....

To be returned not later than Septem
endorsed: "Recreative Physical T
Education Officer, Education Office,
HAM, 3.

P53865 B9 (a) 134/20

CITY OF BIRMINGHAM EDUCATION COMMITTEE

A TWO YEAR

TRAINING COURSE

to prepare Girls and Women aged 16—26 years as

INSTRUCTOR-LEADERS

of

PHYSICAL RECREATION

will commence Autumn, 1946 at
THE PHYSICAL TRAINING CENTRE
(Harborne)
and
THE BIRMINGHAM ATHLETIC INSTITUTE
(Temporary Premises—Severn Street Gymnasium)

The Course will meet on one evening a week and will continue for two years. Opportunity to act as Voluntary Trainee Leaders with Groups and Classes will be arranged during the Course.

PRACTICAL LEADERSHIP TRAINING WILL INCLUDE:

Outdoor Pursuits
Games (Netball, Hockey, Tennis, Rounders, etc.).
"Hiking," Youth Hostel Activities.
Country Rambles, Cycling.
Camping and Climbing.
Swimming. Athletics.
Umpiring.

Indoor Fitness Activities
Keep Fit—Dancing (Modern Dance, National and Character Dancing, Folk Dancing).
Simple Recreative Gymnastics.
Indoor Games.
Skipping, Hoop and Ball Work to Music.

Leadership Practice.

The Theoretical Background of certain forms of Physical Recreation and Elementary Health Education will be studied. Discussions on Social Service and Physical Recreation and observation of Physical Training and Recreation in Schools and Recreative Classes will be arranged. A nominal fee of 7/6 per year will be charged.

E. L. RUSSELL,
Chief Education Officer.

P.T.O. for Enrolment Form.

Advertisement for the Junior Leaders' Training Course 1946

and only the lack of suitable accommodation in the centre of the city prevented the number of students being even greater. Students were being turned away from the men's classes. An extension to the BAI was planned with an additional gymnasium. A sum of £8,000 was allocated, £4,000 to be spent in 1931 − 32 and £4,000 in 1932 − 33. This plan was never implemented. A new plan was put forward which involved the division of the existing gym into two smaller gymnasia with a large gymnasium being built above these two. The estimated cost was £9,500. These alterations were not carried out, and by 1936 Anne Thorpe was writing to Mr Deacon about the acute lack of accommodation. She refers to the scheme prepared in 1931 and states that it would not meet present day needs. She suggested instead, that a central site be acquired which should contain three gymnasia, changing rooms, showers and common room suggesting a site at the back of the Bristol Street School in Bow Street. In addition, alterations to the BAI were suggested which included a new floor. Miss Thorpe also advocated the termination of the BAC's tenancy on Tuesdays and Fridays. It seems that the Club was not recruiting enough members and consequently the BAI was under-used on those nights. These suggestions were not accepted by the Sites and Buildings Sub Committee, but it notes in the 1937 Report that a scheme of alterations was approved and the plans forwarded to the Board of Education. Despite this Anne Thorpe was once again writing to Mr Deacon on 29 September 1937 complaining that Mrs Harper found it very difficult to cope with the influx of enrolments in the cramped conditions. Enrolments were very high with 90 for the Keep Fit classes on Monday evening and 150 for the later class; 150 enrolled for National Dancing, 79 for tap dancing and 88 for ballroom dancing. Students were having to change in the corridors because the cloakrooms were completely inadequate. This extract from her memo illustrates some of the problems:

"It is absolutely essential that Mrs Harper should be free to supervise the classes which are held in three different gymnasia and be able to interview students, and it is hoped that she will not be without Mr Buttriss or a deputy so near the beginning of the session without some intimation. Had I known I should have arranged that either Miss Potts or myself went down as an emergency measure. The need for additional gymnasia is becoming more and more urgent."

Following the 1937 Act there was greater involvement of the BAI in training physical recreation leaders. Anne Thorpe had felt the need for a city-wide

Demonstration teams with Anne Thorpe and Eileen Harper

scheme of physical recreation for women in post school daytime and evening classes. They were the first long-term schemes for training women specifically for work in adult education in Birmingham. Two one-year courses were run 1940 – 42 for women already teaching, but 1942 saw the introduction of two-year courses aimed at 16 year olds and upwards who then went on as leaders in physical recreation. A parallel course was already being run for men. The women's classes proved to be very successful and between 1942 – 1967, 190 leaders were trained.

In the month leading up to the second world war Eileen Harper, along with Anne Thorpe, was responsible for organising 'Pageant of Fitness' for King George the Sixth and Queen Elizabeth. The demonstration took place on 1st

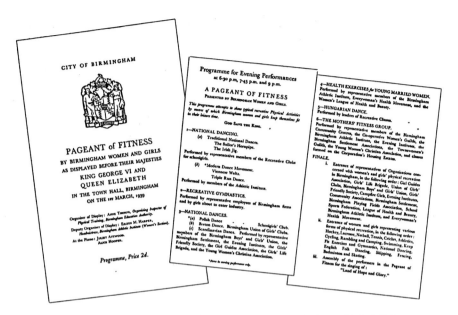

The visit of King George 6th & Queen Elizabeth Town Hall 1939

March 1939 at the Town Hall, and was intended to show typical exercises by which Birmingham women and girls kept themselves fit in their leisure time. The performance included national dance, gymnastics, exercises for young married women and mothers.

The biggest blow during the war was the death, in 1943, of Mrs Eileen Harper, Head of the Women's Section since 1937. Miss Waterman commented in her 1944 Annual Report:-

"Mrs Harper had become an outstanding leader in the cause of physical recreation, not only in our Institute but in the country generally. Her vivacity, encouragement to newcomers, interest in the advanced work of older students attracted students of all grades of society and degree of skill, ... It is our intention to carry on the Institute's work in the spirit and standard which its first woman head has set us".

Miss Waterman did indeed carry on Eileen Harper's work and took the BAI Women's Section to new heights. She had been a full-time teacher since 1942 and was appointed full-time Head in 1944.

Irene Waterman Principal Women's Dept B.A.I. 1944–1975

Inevitably the war curtailed the activities of the BAI because of conscription, the blackout, civil defense and overtime. The building in John Bright Street was bombed by a land mine in 1940. The Institute continued in premises in Severn Street, the first Adult School Union. Clothing rationing caused a shortage of costumes for the various productions and in 1944 a fund was set up to purchase special materials. The April 1944 – March 1945 session saw the largest number of enrolments since the beginning of the war. Inevitably most of the enrolments were young people. The Institute continued to attract a high standard of staff with the arrival of Miss Horley from Chelsea Physical Training College. Other staff left to work at Kings Norton Grammar School whilst one of the pianists joined ENSA.

The return to civilian life saw a further upsurge in women's leisure pursuits and by 1945 enrolments to the Women's Section exceeded 1,000. Women had taken an active role during the war and many were keen to continue. Additional gymnasia were desperately needed to enable the Institute to present its work professionally, to extend the range of activities, to cater for increasing enrolments and to hold classes on more than three evenings a week.

Some of the Lingiad team 1949

Miss Waterman was particularly interested in promoting both the classes for married women and the newly introduced ballet classes. A production group was formed to perform modern dance ballets — ''Everyman'', ''Merry Wives of Windsor'', ''Facade'' and ''the Firebird Suite'' being among the first performances. July 1945 saw three performances at the Midland Institute to show some of the work of intermediate and advanced women's classes. The

44

*Anne Thorpe being presented to HRH Princess Elizabeth at the Villa Park Stadium
1951*

Eileen M Harper Memorial Fund was set up in 1945 to encourage young
students and leaders in their work. Awards, not exceeding £5.00, were made
and some monies were used to buy books for the Institute's Library. The bad
weather in 1947 saw Miss Waterman pleading for doors to be fixed on the
Entrance to cut out the draughts. With considerable foresight she also asked
for a crèche for the children of married women on Monday and Wednesday
afternoons, a goal that has still not been achieved today in many sports
centres.

In 1947 the joint demonstrations of the Men's and Women's Sections
resumed at the Central Hall. In an important initiative, the Institute began to
encourage mixed classes and outdoor games.

The BAI's importance in a national and international context soon became
reestablished. The International Congress of Physical Education held in
London in July 1948 (prior to the Olympic Games), gave the Women's

Trampolining

Section the opportunity to put on a demonstration which was enthusiastically received. International contacts continued with visits from Physical Education Advisers from Australia and Germany.

In 1948, the Women's Section of the Birmingham Athletic Institute was the only team selected to represent Great Britain in the Women's Recreative Physical Training category of the Lingiad World Physical Education Festival

Dance from Prince Igor

in Stockholm, 27 – 31 July 1949. The Lingiad was held every 10 years and was regarded as the gymnastics' counterpart of the Olympic Games, although it was for demonstration rather than competitive.

Miss Waterman led a party of 20 young women. They were accompanied by Miss Anne Thorpe and by their pianist, E Hooper. The team travelled by sea, preferring the Swedish Lloyd Line because many parents expressed misgivings about air travel. The team performed at an indoor demonstration at 11 am on 28 July and again at 3 pm on 30 July. Their routines consisted of skipping and movement using hoops.

After a year of work on the complicated problem of reconstruction, the premises in John Bright Street were reopened by the Minister of Education, the Rt Hon George Tomlinson, MP, at the commencement of the Autumn term, 28th October, 1950. After the cramped conditions at Severn Street the appreciation of the students in the new building was demonstrated by the full

City of Birmingham Education Committee

THE BIRMINGHAM ATHLETIC
INSTITUTE

OFFICIAL OPENING OF THE
RECONSTRUCTED PREMISES
IN JOHN BRIGHT STREET
by the

Rt. Hon. GEORGE TOMLINSON, M.P.
Minister of Education

on SATURDAY, 28th OCTOBER, 1950
at 2.30 p.m.

E. L. RUSSELL · CHIEF EDUCATION OFFICER

The Official re-opening of the John Bright St Premises 1951

Activities for all men

enrolment at classes. The spacious ground floor gymnasium in particular proved to be ideal for large elementary classes of between 80 – 100 students, and made it possible to develop further types of activity, for example badminton. The John Bright and Severn Street premises were used throughout the week on alternate evenings by the Men's and Women's Departments.

The summer term of 1951 was especially eventful, over 21 performances being given in connection with the Festival of Britain programme. On 9th June 100 women students took part in a massed Keep-Fit demonstration during an afternoon of Movement, Dance and Sport at the Villa Park Ground before HRH Princess Elizabeth, soon to become Queen. Advanced students took part in the International Festival of Movement given in the Central Hall in July, together with teams from Finland and Sweden.

January 1956 saw BBC television cameras among the classes, filming for a programme about the work of the BAI. A wide range of activities was shown, from gymnastics to archery, dry-ski-ing and climbing to fencing and ballet ("Prince Igor"). The commentator noted that over 5,000 men and women from every walk of life had enrolled for classes the previous year,

Activities for all women

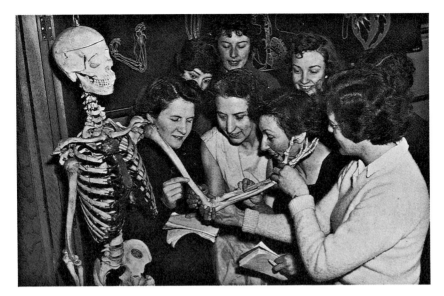

Leaders in training

demonstrating the high reputation of the Institute and fulfillment of its primary object of serving the needs of the people of Birmingham in the spirit of its founders.

Following the formation in September 1957 of the City of Birmingham Physical Recreation Association, the Women's Department of the BAI organised a Festival of Movement, Dance and Sport to be held in the Central Hall, Corporation Street, in May 1958, to consolidate the Association and obtain funds for future activities. The hall was packed to capacity for both performances and 300 students from Evening Institutes and BAI classes gave demonstrations of their work. After 70 years the BAI was therefore flourishing, and had extended and improved its facilities, not only in the centre of Birmingham, but also further afield, using the Education Committee's Training Centre at Harborne with its playing fields and hard tennis courts, and Edgbaston Reservoir for sailing. The indoor programme now included modern, classical and folk dance, judo, weight training, fencing, wrestling and gymnastics, and outdoor sports were hockey, football, netball, tennis, rock-climbing, archery, sub-aqua, dry skiing and sailing. Students from the Institute continued to patronise the training courses for Leaders of Physical Recreation organised by the Education Committee and thus was ensured a supply of high quality leaders for Institutes of Further Education and voluntary organisations. Annual reports reveal that the cost of maintaining the Institute during, for instance, the year 1958 − 59, after the deduction of fee income, was about £18,300. However, the annual reports also plead for more space and more facilities, for although the standards achieved were extremely high, as teams or individuals continued to demonstrate at home and abroad, it was felt that more could be achieved and a larger number of students accommodated if only certain improvements could be made to existing buildings and expansion undertaken where space was available. ''The Institute values highly its position in the centre of the city, which makes it truly a centre for physical recreation for the city as a whole. It is, however, looking forward to the day when this unique centre can be housed in premises more appropriate to the high quality of its work''.

Nevertheless membership was higher than ever, even with the competition offered by increasing ownership of television sets. 1959 saw the purchase of a new 12′ clinker-built sailing dinghy, so that 32 new women students were enrolled for sailing. The married women's classes remained popular, especially those in the late evening. The afternoon classes welcomed young children accompanying their mothers. Several members of these classes continued to appear in the Keep-Fit programme with Eileen Fowler in the

Dancing in Munich

'Mainly for Women' BBC TV series. Classical ballet was steadily increasing its enrolment, the rigorous and highly disciplined training meeting a demand among the students, many of whom took external examinations, all with honours.

In February 1959 Miss Waterman was approached by the Chairman of the Children and Families World Community Chest to take a team of dancers to Munich's Refugee Village to celebrate in a Festival of Dance the opening of playing fields for the children. Ten men and women travelled to Munich for a week's visit and gave five performances of Irish and English 17th century dances. The visit to the refugee camp which housed 23 different nationalities was most memorable and many friends were made.

The sport of gymnastics, which was a dominating infuence in the BAC, out of which grew the BAI, was once again coming to the fore under the instruction of Bernard Thomas and on 9th April 1960, an inspired BAI team made gymnastics history by beating the 'unbeatable' Army School of Physical Training Team, and so once again winning the coveted Adam Shield.

But conditions were deteriorating and annual reports renew their pleas for

The Adams Shield team

Anne Thorpe's retirement

21 dancing years—now pupils' children join in

WED.
27 Dec.
1967.

Few can claim to have begun their life in a trunk at the side of a stage, but for some Birmingham schoolchildren there is an element of truth in the words.

They are the children whose stage-struck mothers were members of the Birmingham Dance Group and who regularly took them along to the weekly classes and exercising at the parallel bars.

The Birmingham Dance Group, the only one of its kind in the country, is celebrating its 21st birthday this year and for the principal, Miss Irene Waterman, the occasion brings more than the usual share of nostalgia.

"In a few months, I shall be enrolling the children of my first pupils," she said. "My first pupils came from many walks of life, but many were housewives with small children.

"Everyone said I was mad and that I would never get any adult to take up ballet, but how wrong they were," Miss Waterman said. "Usually, I have about 20 in my juniors class, which depends on dancing experience, not age, and the same in my dance group."

Miss Waterman became Principal of the Women's Department of the Birming-

Birmingham Post Reporter

ham Athletic Institute, where the Dance Group classes are held, in 1944. In 1946, she founded classes for modern dance and classical ballet.

Miss Waterman quickly dispelled the fallacy that at a certain age, the muscles of the body are so stiff from lack of exercise that you can never be a dancer.

"Rubbish," she said, "if a woman between 16 and 25 comes to me with no previous dancing experience but the correct physique and determination, I can make those muscles supple again."

Minimum age for admission to the dance classes is 15, but the oldest member is well over 40.

At present, the group is giving a series of Christmas dance performances at the Institute in Severn Street, Birmingham.

Several members have become professional dancers and probably the most successful is 18-year-old Margaret Burton, the caretaker's daughter, now training at the Royal Ballet School in London.

"She was admitted to our classes very much under age at ten," Miss Waterman said, "but she showed exceptional talent. Then, when she was

12, she was auditioned for the school and was accepted immediately."

In many of the productions, which have ranged from *Sleeping Beauty* to *Pineapple Poll*, the male parts have been taken by female members.

"But once or twice, men from the men's department gymnastics class have shown an interest and volunteered to train for a part," Miss Waterman said. "They have done very well, too, but not many return for a second time. They say that ballet is far too strenuous for them."

Newspaper cutting "21 dancing years"

improvements. It was stressed that students would not continue to enrol at the Institute when superior modern buildings were available at schools and local institutes. A multi-purpose sports hall was urgently needed, and it was hoped that the city that had taken the lead in 1890 would rise to the challenge and provide its specialist Institute with facilities to achieve the highest possible standard. Severn Street at last received its new canteen in September 1961 and it was greatly appreciated by the students attending classes there.

April 1961 and another visit abroad, this time to Holland. Miss Anne Thorpe, had attended a world conference on 'Physical Recreation outside

Margaret Burton in training at B.A.I.

School' in the Hague the previous year, as a result of which a team from Birmingham was invited to demonstrate physical recreation in Velsen, Gronigon, Arnhem and Amersfoort. 26 leaders, BAI members and teachers gave a performance of very high standard lasting an hour and which included Keep Fit, Skipping, Ball-movement, Irish and Scottish dancing, Modern dance and Court dances of England. During the ten days in Holland the team was welcomed and lived in the houses of Dutch families. At Arnhem a wreath was placed on the Cenotaph and the graves of the Birmingham men who gave their lives in the 2nd World War were visited. The tour was a great success, a happy and enjoyable experience for all who took part.

The Finnish Fortnight celebrations in Birmingham, in February 1964, gave an opportunity for foreign visitors to the BAI to demonstrate their skills. The Suomi girls, a Finnish gymnastic group, gave several performances in Birmingham and were enthusiastically received.

To mark the retirement of Miss Thorpe, Organising Inspector of Physical

Visit of the HRH the Duke of Edinburgh to see his award scheme in operation 1970

Education for Birmingham since 1931, a three-day Summer Festival was staged at the BAI in July 1966. Each day the programme was different — movement training was emphasised on the first day, sport on the second, and dance on the final day. In all 700 people took part including primary and secondary school children, young adults and older women. At each performance Miss Thorpe was presented with a gift token and a scroll signed by each of the participants. For the past 35 years Miss Thorpe had inspired teachers and leaders with her enthusiasm, far-sightedness and wealth of knowledge, together with her understanding of human nature and her love of children, and this Festival, attended by her friends and colleagues, was a fitting tribute to her from the BAI, which she strongly supported throughout her career.

A co-operative effort to make an impact on the people of Birmingham was undertaken in the summer of 1967 by the BAI and the Institutes of Further Education, when an Exhibition of Physical Recreation for Adults was mounted in the Centre Court of the Bull Ring. Demonstrations of physical activities were given during a week in June and members of the public were invited to participate. Large crowds watched a fashion parade of sports clothes and queued to take part in activities, the most popular of which was undoubtedly trampolining.

Certainly enrolment numbers and attendances remained good, though lack of accommodation remained a serious problem, making any attempt at expansion a frustrating task. A few statistical facts on the women's classes might be of interest. During the year 1967 — 68 over two-thirds of the students were aged 21 years and over, ages ranging from 15 to 70 years, and of these the overwhelming majority were office-workers, though three years later the office workers comprised only 30%. Hours spent on the 32 different activities on offer show Keep-Fit a strong favourite, and including a few token males. Specialist Staff were paid at the rate of 41/4d per hour, but 82/8d for three hours! — about 20% above staff in other Adult Education Centres. The figures, as always, show clearly that the Institute catered for a cross section of the population and served its fundamental purpose of providing Physical Recreation for the citizens of Birmingham.

But Miss Waterman writes in 1966: "It is impossible to expand effectively with the present accommodation. People who do find their way to the Institute find very specialised work and a high standard of teaching, coupled with a friendly, informal atmosphere. However, considering the size of Birmingham and its population, the Institute is touching a pathetically small proportion of the public. Hundreds of people have never heard of the BAI. Those who know it well consider it to be an integral part of their lives. An Institute with a history of 77 years behind it is deserving of a much more prominent place in the cultural and recreational life of the city. This will only be possible with much better facilities."

Expansion seemed burdened with difficulties. And there were other worries: "There is evidence that many of the activities which hitherto were only available at this Institute are now being offered in the local Adult Education Centres — eg. mountaineering, sailing, Yoga, hockey. It must be admitted that many of the new schools offer far better facilities than can at present be offered by this Institute. In addition, there is no added expense of bus fares into the city centre ... or problems over parking. If the policy of the Education Committee is to develop recreative activities locally then this Institute is bound to suffer from every point of view ... the possibility of the new building appears to be as remote as it has ever been. No freedom is given for the Institute to branch out into non-physical activities and yet the local Institutes have complete freedom to develop the physical side of their

FROM STRENGTH TO STRENGTH

Final Leaders' Training Course run by the Birmingham Education Authority 1972/74

Institutes as far as they can''. And the following year: ''No official information about the new building has been received during the past year. No help has been offered to staff for the parking of their cars ... increased bus fares, lack of parking for students' cars, poor facilities compared with new local schools, development of specialist sporting activities in local Institutes, all aim at reducing support for BAI classes. A new look at the way the Institute can best serve the community at the present time is absolutely essential.''

But work continued as usual. In November 1970 the BAI Women's Department represented Further Education when the Duke of Edinburgh visited Lewis's Department Store to see an exhibition of work by boys and girls engaged in his award scheme. In May of the following year many extra hours of work by the staff resulted in a very high standard of performance, both in the New Street Station Concourse every day and, on Wednesday evening, at the Central Hall, as part of the ''Explode 71'' Youth Festival. The programme included gymnastics, trampolining, dance, weight training,

EXPLODE 1971

"VIVA PERFECTION"

THE
BIRMINGHAM ATHLETIC INSTITUTE
and SCHOOL CLUBS

PRESENT

AN EXPLOSION OF MOVEMENT

at

The CENTRAL HALL, Corporation Street

on

26th MAY, 1971, at 7.15 p.m.

Activities include Gymnastics, Trampolining, Dance, Weight Training, Aikido, Skipping, combined to give a Kaleidoscope of movement and colour

TICKETS   **25 p** (5/-)   **15 p** (3/-)   **10 p** (2/-)

Obtainable from :

The B.A.I., John Bright Street, Birmingham 1

Telephone :   Men's Department—643 5440

Women's Department—643 1113

or City Information Office, Council House, Birmingham

A. A. Ladbrook & Son, Printers, Bordesley, Birmingham 12.

Explode 71 Advertisement

61

ACTIVITY	DAY	VENUE
Aikido	Monday, Tuesday, Thursday, Friday	John Bright and Severn Street
Athletics	Monday, Tuesday, Thursday	Holloway Head
Badminton	Monday, Wednesday, Thursday, Saturday	John Bright Street
Ball Games	Monday, Friday	Severn Street and St. Alban's School
Ball Movements	Tuesday, Wednesday, Thursday	John Bright Street and Severn Street
Ballroom Dancing	Tuesday	Severn Street
Businessmen's Keep Fit	Monday, Tuesday, Thursday, Friday	John Bright and Severn Street
Classical Ballet	Monday, Wednesday, Thursday, Saturday	John Bright and Severn Street
Fencing	Monday, Wednesday	Severn Street
Fitness for Skiing	Tuesday	Severn Street
Football	Wednesday, Thursday, Sunday,	Metchley Lane
Gymnastics (Basic for Women)	Monday	Johr Bright Street
Hockey	Saturday, Thursday	Metchley Lane Fields and Severn Street
Hoop Movements and Skipping	Tuesday, Friday	Severn Street
International Folk Dance	Wednesday	John Bright Street
Karate	Saturday	Severn Street
Judo (Women)	Thursday, Friday	Severn Street
Judo (Men)	Monday, Wednesday, Thursday	Severn and John Bright Street
Keep Fit (Women)	Monday, Tuesday, Wednesday, Thursday	John Bright and Severn Street
Modern Dance	Wednesday, Friday	John Bright and Severn Street
Modern Jazz Ballet	Monday, Thursday	John Bright and Severn Street
Mountaineering	Thursday	John Bright Street
Movement for the Elderly	Tuesday, Wednesday	John Bright Street
Keep Fit for Retireds	Tuesday, Wednesday	John Bright Street
National Dance	Tuesday, Wednesday, Thursday	John Bright and Severn Street
Netball	Thursday, Friday, Saturday	John Bright Street and Blessed Humphrey Middlemoore School, Holloway Head
Olympic Gymnastics (Women)	Wednesday	John Bright Street
Olympic Gymnastics (Men)	Monday, Tuesday, Thursday, Saturday	John Bright Street
Physical Activities (Men)	Thursday	John Bright Street
Sailing	Monday, Tuesday, Wednesday, Thursday, Friday	Brookvale Park Reservoir
Scottish Dance	Monday	John Bright Street
Skipping	Monday, Tuesday, Wednesday, Thursday	John Bright and Severn Street
Sub-Aqua	Wednesday	Green Lane Baths
Spanish Dance	Monday	John Bright Street
Swimming	Tuesday, Thursday	Greve Lane and Green Lane Baths
Tennis	Monday, Wednesday, Friday, Saturday	Metchley Lane Fields and Holloway Head
Table Tennis	Friday	Severn Street
Trampolining	Monday, Tuesday, Wednesday, Thursday, Friday	John Bright Street
Tumbling and Mini-Tramp.	Friday	John Bright Sreet
Volleyball	Tuesday	Lea Mason School
Wrestling (Olympic)	Monday, Friday	John Bright and Severn Street
Yoga	Monday, Tuesday, Wednesday, Thursday, Friday	Severn Street and John Bright Street
Dance Group	Friday	Severn Street
Weight Training	Monday, Wednesday, Thursday, Friday	Severn Street

1974 Programme of Activities

aikido, and skipping, "combined to give a Kaleidoscope of movement and colour".

July 1975 saw the retirement of Miss Waterman, Principal of the Women's Department. Writing her last annual report, Miss Waterman reminisces on the past 33 years since 1942 when she arrived as a member of the full-time staff. It was wartime, and enrolment for the first term was 206 students in 16 classes and Miss Waterman is justly satisfied with the equivalent numbers in her last year of office — 3,501 students and 108 classes, a record number for both. However, she records her disappointment that the Institute was to revert to a mixed Institute as she believes that the Women's Department had benefited from separation from the Men's and developed differently. Her Parthian shot is a typical plea for splendid new facilities, "the Second City in England should have them and the citizens need them".

In January 1976 the Education Committee approved a recommendation that from 1st September, 1975, the BAI should be recognised as a single

Eric Bates Principal of the Mens' department with his team of gymnasts

establishment by merging the Men's and Women's Departments, thus reverting to the original arrangement. Eric Bates, Principal of the Men's Department since 1947, was appointed Principal of the unified Institute, and after almost a year of uncertainty and debate it was finally decided not to create a post of Vice-Principal, but to organise the institute in two departments and appoint Miss Barbara Thomas as head of the Women's Department and Barry Benn as head of the Men's Department.

After the retirement of Eric Bates in 1977 various discussions to consider the work and future of the BAI were held by the Department of Education and early in 1978 Kerry Mumford was appointed as the new Principal. Although the present outstanding and important function of the BAI in Adult Recreation with special reference to groups of above average ability or particular interests was to continue, the remit of the new Principal included increasing the use of the BAI both at weekends and during the day by other bona-fide groups, in co-operation with governing bodies of sport and the Sports Council. It was also envisaged that the Institute should develop holiday courses and play a major part in the 'Holiday Project Scheme' already operating in the City, extend co-operation with the Physical Education Inspectorate in the present role of leader and teacher training and, finally, develop 'Centres of Excellence' as defined by the Sports Council. These developments in the work of the BAI were necessitated to meet changes in the demand and needs for Physical Recreation and Sport in the City.

Metchley Lane Centre had already been in use by the BAI for some time now as a specialist gymnastics centre and discussions re-opened regarding use of the Aston Manor site to act as an alternative to Severn Street where "water was now coming through the roof and flooding stairways and toilets as well as seeping close to electrical switches" and the ceiling in the weight training room had fallen in. Closure of Severn Street seemed increasingly to be a possibility and Aston Manor appeared to offer a solution as one of the few sites which could accommodate a substantial programme of activities and therefore sustain the particular camaraderie of the Institute. As Kerry Mumford pointed out in a memorandum dated 29th September 1980, "The BAI, as the City's major establishment for sporting excellence, does not have one full size facility under its control for any activity for which the Sports Council recommends an appropriate size. We succeed regardless!" Several attempts had already been made to include replacement premises for the BAI in building programmes. It was to have been included in the Paradise Circus development; considerable design work was undertaken to include it in a proposed Snow Hill development; attempts were made to have specialist accommodation included in private city-centre developments; but at the end of 1980 there was still little likelihood of purpose build accommodation being erected in the foreseeable future. At last a solution was found. In recognition of the quality of work done and the growing numbers of students, the then leader of the City Council, Councillor Clive Wilkinson, made provision for the replacement of the Headquarters in John Bright Street by authorising the building of a new complex and headquarters.

The BAI was to be accommodated both in the existing Highgate Community Centre and in a new Sports Hall building adjacent to it. Specialist sporting facilities were to be provided in the new building, while the Community Centre would provide facilities for local youth and community groups and the BAI administration offices. The new building was constructed in modern materials and employed up-to-date techniques to achieve a short construction period and commensurate economy. The large steel roof covered

CITY OF BIRMINGHAM DISTRICT COUNCIL

Official Opening

of
THE NEW HEADQUARTERS
of the
BIRMINGHAM ATHLETIC INSTITUTE
HIGHGATE, BIRMINGHAM B12 9DL
by

H.R.H. The Duke of Edinburgh K.G., K.T.

on
TUESDAY 26th JULY 1983

Official opening of the Highgate Building 1983 by HRH The Duke of Edinburgh

an area of 2,000 sq.m., supported by a steel portal frame with a span of 45 m. The Sports Hall itself was high enough for all indoor ball games; it and the gymnasia were equipped for sport to international standards and the Sports Hall was able to seat up to 600 spectators on special occasions. Rooms for judo, wrestling and other martial arts were included, also a weight-training room and a general purpose hall with seats for 200 and the capability of sub-division for lectures and demonstrations. Sustenance for participants was provided by a coffee bar and a licensed bar connecting the new building with the Community Centre, enhancing the social atmosphere and club feeling. The new complex and headquarters of the BAI was officially opened on 26th July, 1983, by HRH the Duke of Edinburgh and, in combination with the recently opened Astroturf pitch outside the new facilities, made the Highgate campus a unique sporting asset for the City.

A year later, in April 1984, within the general reorganisation of City Departments, the BAI was transferred from the Education Department to the Recreation & Community Services Department, when this latter Department took responsibility for sport as well as adult education. By this time the BAI was operating at 6 different sites around the city — the Highgate headquarters, the Dance Centre at the Hippodrome, Metchley Lane, Aston Manor, Holloway Head playing fields and Brookvale Park Sailing Centre, demonstrating without doubt that the BAI was not just a building, but more a concept, with its own very special spirit. It had continued to function for its original purpose as an adult education establishment, with special reference to groups of above average ability or with special needs and where special equipment was needed, but had also broadened its horizons, as requested in 1978, to develop youth work, introducing more weekend and holiday courses and early evening specialist courses for those who showed potential. The Institute co-ordinated the administration for the Tarmac School of Sport, a scheme whereby 130 of the best children in Birmingham were coached intensively during the Christmas and Easter holidays. Another newer function, the development of centres of excellence, continued unabated, often with extra voluntary coaching by the staff in order to maintain standards of performance. Increasingly, due to the expertise of the staff, they were heavily involved in In Service Training of School Teachers and the Youth Service. Many schools used the BAI premises, and BAI staff helped in schools as part of the schools' curriculum 'life and leisure' courses.

Additional schemes in which the BAI played a significant part were the Physical Education Advisory Service to Adult Education Youth and Community, the National Coaching Foundation, the Birmingham Schools

Sports Federation, Action Sport and inter-institute youth activities programmes. Two Centres of Excellence were established in the Institute in conjunction with their Governing Bodies — Table Tennis and Badminton — and the BAI continued to publicise its work both in its annual Spectacular Display held at the end of each year and by visits to clubs, schools, carnivals and major shows. Throughout the years the excellence of the training produced an exceptional number of internationals, something of a tradition at the BAI, but the special BAI ethos and atmosphere enabled the beginner and high level performer to work together, many of the beginner level classes being taught by the same highly qualified and experienced coaches responsible for producing international sportsmen and women.

In 1984 and 1985 the City of Birmingham inaugurated organisation and performance reviews. As a result of the first review, the BAI was moved from Education to Recreation & Community Services. The BAI presented its views on its future role. Basically it envisaged playing a major part as a Sports Development Unit, co-ordinating opportunities for more people to take part in sport and ensuring that those people who wished had the opportunity to improve their skills. These proposals were perhaps too ambitious and therefore failed to win support. Finance was possibly the overriding factor that determined the final decision. By October 1984 the BAI in name no longer existed. The Highgate complex was re-named the Birmingham Sports Centre and its staffing structure changed to bring it into line with other centres under the aegis of the Recreation & Leisure Services Department. The other sites used by the old BAI were re-allocated and although the new sports centre was still doing many of the things that the BAI had done, it was not all housed in one building. The 1983/84 brochure was the last which spelt out the history and functions of the Institute as an introduction to the courses on offer and the brochure for the year 1987/88 is the final one published under the name Birmingham Athletic Institute.

LANDMARKS IN THE HISTORY OF THE BIRMINGHAM ATHLETIC INSTITUTE

1844   The Athenic Institute founded.

1866   The Birmingham Athletic Club founded to further gymnastics, athletics and all branches of physical culture. Clement Davies appointed first Chairman of the BAC Committee. Joseph Hubbard appointed first instructor.

1868   BAC created The Birmingham Gymnasium Building Fund.

1870   George Dixon appointed Chairman of the Birmingham School Board.

1879   George Dixon pressed for physical recreation and training on elementary school curriculum.

1880   Ten members of the BAC competed in the International Gymnastics Competition at Frankfurt-on-Main. Twenty thousand gymnasts took part in front of 150,000 spectators.
George Dixon collaborated with Professor Hubbard to develop a scheme of Physical Education in Board Schools and provide in-service training for teachers.

1883   Birmingham School Board Physical Exercises Committee promoted by George Dixon, Chaired by George Kenrick.

1886   School Board proposed the introduction of daily physical exercise in Board Schools. Physical Exercises Committee to appoint a full-time instructor to train teachers.

1887   Athletic Festival in Town Hall to celebrate the BAC's 21st anniversary.

1887   Inauguration of the National Physical Recreation Society — "to bring fresh air, exercise and sport within the reach of the people ..." BAC first club to join.

1888   Lord Beresford's major address to the 22nd annual Festival of the BAC.

1889   BAC Committee launched a city wide appeal to establish a city gymnasium.

October. BAC Special Committee promoted the establishment of an institution — The Birmingham Athletic Institute.

24 October 1889. The Mayor, Alderman Barrow called a public meeting at Council House at which George Kenrick proposed "... to establish in Birmingham an institution for the promotion of physical education under the name of the Birmingham Athletic Institute".

Henry Mitchell became the first President; Prof Hubbard became the first Director.

1890   General Committee of the BAC canvassed the city for subscribers.

The Birmingham School Board's Physical Exercises Committee's responsibilities to be transferred to the BAI.

1891   Inauguration by BAI Council of a Committee of Management of Physical Exercises in Elementary Schools to promote city wide physical education in Board Schools.

Health lectures inaugurated.

May. Building commenced on the John Bright Street Site. Sports ground acquired at Pershore Road.

1892   26 February. George Kenrick offered the BAI Council the John Bright Street premises which he had built and furnished at his own expense for little or no rent for a period of five years from 1 January 1892.

27 February. BAI premises officially opened by the Attorney General Sir Richard Webster MP.

1894   Deputy Director appointed — Professor Clease to supervise day-time classes.

1896   Professor Hubbard resigns from Institute.

First all-ladies display presented in Town Hall.

Institute recognised BAI as training centre for teachers of physical exercise in elementary schools.

1897   Team of young ladies gave a demonstration in Dublin under the personal patronage of Countess Plunkett.

BAI and BAC collaborated to give a demonstration in the Birmingham Jubilee Procession.

1898   Board of Education produced a full length report on the Institute's scheme for organisation of extra-curricular games in schools. Recommended that other industrial cities would do well to follow suit.

1899   BAI established a unit for remedial work with students with physical defects.

Student teachers from the Birmingham Day Teacher Training College for Men received regular physical training classes.

1902   Surprise visit to BAI by the Lord Chief Justice of England who as Sir Richard Webster had officiated at the opening.

George Kenrick elected to the Education Committee.

1909   George Kenrick knighted.

1910   New responsibilities were given to the Birmingham Athletic Institute concerning the training of teachers.

The BAI relinquished the use of the playing fields on the Pershore Road.

1914   Death of Henry Mitchell.

1916   BAI made a severe loss. Death of Professor Hubbard.

1917   George Kenrick offered the BAI building and playing fields on the Pershore Road to the Education Committee Birmingham Corporation.

1937   The BAI was divided into two separate departments, and a Head of Women's Section appointed.

1939   "Pageant of Fitness" by Birmingham Women and Girls before George VI and Queen Elizabeth. Death of George Kenrick.

1940   BAI was bombed and sought temporary accommodation in Severn Street.

1942   2 year, part-time training courses for leaders of physical recreation were introduced.

1946   The affairs of the BAC were wound up.

1948   BAI performed at the 1948 International Council for Sport and Physical Education Conference.

1949   20 girls from the BAI Women's Department represented Great Britain at the "Lingiad" in Sweden.

1950   Official opening of reconstructed premises in John Bright Street by George Tomlinson, MP, Minister for Education.

1951   Display of Physical Recreation, Villa Park, 9th June, as part of Festival of Britain celebrations.

1956   BAI features on BBC TV programme, 5 January.

1958   1st Festival of Movement, Dance & Sport at Central Hall, Corporation Street.

1959   Visit to Munich Refugee Village on the Initiation of the Children & Families World Community Chest.

1961 BAI invited to tour Holland to demonstrate 'physical recreation outside school.'
1964 BAI took part in the Finnish Fortnight celebrations in Birmingham.
1966 Summer Festival to mark retirement of Anne Thorpe, Organising Inspector of Physical Education, 1931 – 66.
1971 Demonstrations given by BAI as part of 'Explode 71' Youth Festival in Birmingham.
1975 Retirement of Miss Irene Waterman.
1977 Retirement of Mr Eric Bates.
1978 Appointment of Mr Kerry Mumford.
1983 26th July. Opening of new BAI headquarters at Highgate by HRH the Duke of Edinburgh.
1984 April — BAI transferred from Education Department to Recreation & Community Services Department.

BALLETS PRODUCED BY THE BAI DANCE GROUP

1943 The Lady of Shalott
1945 Sacred & Profane
1946 Everyman
1947 Merry Wives of Windsor
      The Pranks of Puck
      Facade
1948 Christina
1949 Gayeneh
1951 La Valse
1952 Scaramouche
1953 Alice in Wonderland
1955 Prince Igor
1956 The Christmas Story
1957 The Players
1958 Anna
1959 Pied Piper of Hamelin
      Sleeping Princess
1960 Carnival
1961 La Boutique Fantasque
      Capriccio Espagnol
      Amahl and the Night Visitors

1962	Love the Magician
1963	Symphony for Fun
1964	Firebird
1965	Romeo & Juliet
1966	Rio Grande
	Midsummer Nights Dream
1967	Pineapple Poll
1968	Petrushka
1969	Jeux d'Enfants
	Mother Goose
1970	Carmina Burana
	Peer Gynt
1971	La Fille Mal Gardee
1972	Cinderella
1973	Coq d'Or
1974	The Lion, the Witch & the Wardrobe
	Rite of Spring
1975	Come Together in Jesus Name

Youth Concerts with the Birmingham Symphony Orchestra

1956	Alexander's Feast
1961	La Boutique Fantasque
	Capriccio Espagnol
1962	Love the Magician
1963	Austrian Peasant Dances
1964	Symphony for Fun
1965	Romeo & Juliet
1966	Midsummer Night's Dream
1967	Pineapple Poll

Dance Produced for Amateur Grand Operas

1963   Zampa
1964   Prince Igor
1967   Jacobin
1972   Idomineo
1973   Aida
1976   La Giaconda
1977   Carmen
1977   Orpheus in the Underworld
1978   Turendot
1980   Pearl Fishers
1982   Eugene Onegin
1984   Force of Destiny
1989   Aida

Classical Ballet

Spanish Dance

Hoop Movement

Keep-Fit

Movement for the retireds

Movement with Balls

Modern Dance

Dance Skipping

Scottish Dance visiting team

Yoga

Netball

Badminton Club 1951 – 52

Olympic Gymnastics

Judo Women's team

Table Tennis

Gymnastics

Judo

Weight Training

Basket Ball

Fencing

The Birmingham Athletic Institute Remembered

Sailing

87

BIBLIOGRAPHY

Bates. Pictorial Guide to Birmingham. Allen & Son. 1849.

Birmingham Athletic Club Original Minute Books. 1866 – 1871
1888 – 1918

Birmingham Athletic Institute Annual Reports. 1891 – 1975

Birmingham Technical Education Committee Minutes. 1918.

Birmingham Faces and Places. Volume 5. J. G. Hammond. 1893.

R. K. Dent. Old and New Birmingham. Houghton & Hammond, 1880.

G. Dixon, M.P. Addresses to the School Board. 1876 – 1888.

A. E. Dobbs. Education & Social Movements, 1700 – 1850. Longmans, Green & Co. 1919.

E. Eaglesham. From School Board to Local Authority. Routledge & Kegan Paul, 1956.

H. J. Edwards. The Evening Institute. National Institute of Adult Education, 1961.

J. F. C. Harrison. Learning & Living. 1790 – 1960. Routledge & Kegan Paul, 1961.

J. W. Hudson. History of Adult Education. Longmore Brown. 1851.

T. Kelly. History of Adult Education in Great Britain. Liverpool University Press, 1962.

J. A. Langford. Modern Birmingham and its Institutions. 1841 – 1871. E. C. Osborne, 1873.

E. L. Levy. History of the Birmingham Athletic Club. 1866 – 1898. J. G. Hammond, 1898.

E. L. Levy. Autobiography of an Athlete. J. G. Hammond, 1913.

E. L. Levy. Pen Pictures of a Popular Past. J. G. Hammond, 1916.

B. Simon. Education & the Labour Movement, 1870 – 1920. Lawrence & Wishart, 1965.

D. Thomson. England in the Nineteenth Century. Penguin Books, 1967.

E. P. Thompson. Making of the English Working Class. Penguin Books, 1968.

West of England Miscellany No. 1. John Churchill, 1844.

M. I. Waterman. The History of the Birmingham Athletic Institute 1866 – 1918 Thesis 1970

Daily Newspapers

Birmingham Daily Gazette. 1868 – 1918.

Birmingham Post. 1902 – 1918.

Weekly Magazine

Sport & Play. 1879 – 1888.

Original sources underlined